1. introduction

In recent years there has been growing interest in West European trade union and political circles about ideas for securing a more equitable sharing in, as well as control of, capital growth in industry through the medium of trade union organisation. It is not surprising that this search which is in the same style as their interest in workers' participation in the management of resources and which amounts to a determination to extend democracy to the economic and industrial field, should have become more active during a period which has seen the emergence of multi-national corporations. To many socialists these now pose the most serious challenge to concepts of democracy in our society and they provide a spur to the unions' quest for new ways of controlling capital and making it more responsive to social needs.

This pronounced demand for economic and industrial democracy has, at the same time, been nourished by the growing rejection by workers generally of any society which is based on significant ineqalities in the distribution of incomes and capital, with a resultant concentration of ownership and decision making amongst a wealthy elite. This rejection is based, in part, on their fundamental disagreement with the view that such a form of society is necessary in order to provide the volume of saving and, therefore, of capital needed to sustain and increase industrial and commercial investment.

Trade unionists and their supporters do not reject the view that there is a pressing need for increased investment in industry. They accept the fact that faster and more stable growth rates, full employment and higher living standards can best be achieved by increased and sustained capital formation. What they do dispute, however, is that this acceptance of an economic fact of life implies an acceptance of antiquated theories about the need for vast concentrations of privately owned wealth in order to provide the finance for new productive investment. Their search has already begun for more modern solutions which will also be a step forward in achieving traditional trade union objectives of greater equality and meaningful participation in industrial decision making.

The purpose of this pamphlet is to make a contribution to that search by setting out a case for an approach to the problem of wealth distribution within which collective bargaining institutions might be used to secure the collective ownership and control—through the medium of trade unions—of the nations' capital structure. The objective is not to provide a detailed blueprint which deals with all problems and eventualities, but to suggest a framework of ideas within which trade union policies could be drawn up.

the dynamics of inequality

Few will reject the assertion that our society has an inequitable distribution of incomes and wealth. Many will, however, have the vague impression that a fairer distribution was—at least until the recent emphasis on means tested benefits took place—being achieved gradually, especially by the building up of a social security element in incomes—the social wage. Yet the most recent Inland Revenue figures (*Inland revenue statistics,* 1970, HMSO), which are based on estate duty statistics and are considered by some to understate the degree of concentration (see A. B. Atkinson, *The distribution of wealth and the individual life cycle,* Oxford Economic Papers, July 1971) show that 17.3 million persons owned the £88,000 million of estimated total net personal wealth in Great Britain during 1968. Nearly one quarter of this colossal fortune (£21,300 million) was still owned by the richest one per cent, while the richest nine per cent owned well over half.

Significantly, just over £18,000 million of this total wealth was held in the form of stocks and shares and this was distributed between a mere 2.4 million owners. However, even this was not the whole story, for half of them (1.3 million) had holdings of less than £1,000 in value. This suggests that the bulk of share ownership, and with it the control of large sectors of industry, is still concentrated narrowly in very few hands. At the other end of the scale, the revenue figures show little or no wealth for over two thirds of the population. Whatever else the sixties may have achieved it obviously made little impression on the distribution and the ownership of wealth.

The shape of incomes distribution follows a similar pattern, although the mere reproduction of statistics does not convey the facts about our incomes. Some attempt to meet this conceptual difficulty was made in a recent book on the subject which envisaged an hour long procession of all income earners in which each person's size was proportionate to their incomes, with those earning above or below average incomes being above or below average height. Not until about twelve minutes before the end was the parade of pygmies over and persons of average height seen. In the final few minutes the giants loomed up (including doctors seven to eight yards high!) and in the last few seconds the really colossal figures appeared whose height was measured in miles (Jan Pen, *Income distribution,* Penguin, 1971). This is an illuminating method of explaining that the distribution of incomes in this country is skewed, that is to say, significantly unequal.

It was undoubtedly facts such as these that led the TUC to press the recent Labour government to introduce a wealth tax to even up this imbalance. It is a matter for regret that this advice was not taken at the time for what now seems to be the invalid reason of pressure of work at the Inland Revenue. This excuse does not seem to have been a problem in carrying out recent socially regressive taxation changes or in the formulation of a value added tax.

The more serious (because the are cumulative) implications of the wealth and income distribution figures is that, while the bulk of property, including the ownership of private industry, is concentrated in the hands of a rich and powerful minority (often operating not as individuals but as largely anonymous, frequently self perpetuating, financial institutions), there is little evidence that this concentration is lessening. The fact that such groups stand to gain considerably from any development which leads to greater profits and, therefore, higher capital appreciation (including any voluntary restraint in price and income movements, encouragement of the retention of profits and the self financing of capital formation) is a major obstacle to the emergence of any trade union support for efforts to recreate a viable incomes policy.

During the recent period covered by the Labour government's prices and incomes policy, it has been agreed that, despite its shortcomings, the rest of the community could look to the efforts of the government by means of the taxation of capital gains, the re-structuring of corporate taxation, the extension of public ownership, changes in social security benefits and other measures, to divert the greater part of any increased profit flow away from existing wealth holders towards communal purposes. But it was also the case that a policy which went out of its way to encourage the retention of profits rather than their distribution, together with the use of public funds averaging £450 million a year to encourage private investment, both made possible greater increases in capital gains and also ensured the payment of enhanced or maintained dividends in the future.

Admittedly, the prices and incomes policy provided for some control over dividends. But the restraints imposed on wealth holders under it were of a different kind to the cruder restrictions laid down for wage earners (just as the recent changes in tax provisions have clearly favoured this former group, compared with wage and salary earners generally). The outcome was a gradual erosion of the faith of trade unions and their members in the help an incomes policy could give them in creating a more equal society.

Linked to this situation has been the increasing reliance of firms on self financed capital investment for industrial expansion, manifesting the enormous demand of modern industry for capital to discover and develop new technologies. Although much of UK industry is currently experiencing a cyclical down turn in investment, it was notable that, during the period when the prices and incomes policy was fully applied, retained company profits financed a greater proportion of fixed capital formation than in the preceding period. As the following table shows, during the period 1968-70, retained company profits averaged £2,895 million a year; this compared with a slightly lower annual average of £2,788 million for the preceding three years. This was more than enough to finance industry's investment in new productive capacity for the total actually spent on fixed capital formation during 1968-70 averaged £2,830 million a year, compared with the previous three years' annual average of £2,353 million.

RETAINED PROFITS AND INVESTMENT

year	total company income (£m)	undistributed profits (£m)	fixed capital formation (£m)
1965	4,174	3,045	2,386
1966	3,654	2,677	2,379
1967	3,700	2,642	2,294
1968	4,544	2,964	2,563
1969	4,849	2,959	2,795
1970	4,789	2,762	3,132

source: *Financial statistics,* HMSO, April 1971.

As the figures above show, the argument that retained profits financed investment was true of every year over the period except for 1970 and this can probably be accounted for by special factors.

The myth that our capital growth is dependent upon the savings of numerous small investors, cannot be sustained in the face of this sort of evidence. The reality is one of large concentrations of financial, economic and political power generating their own capital resources by means of regressive pricing policies and able to divert an increasing share of income and wealth to their own purposes as a result.

It is indeed evident that, even after taking account of changes in money values, a significant proportion of private industry's investment is typically financed out of retained profits. The fact that this increase in the capital wealth of companies is also added to the wealth of existing shareholders (by means of increased share values and capital gains) raises important policy questions about the way the effects of such auto-financing of investment on the distribution of incomes and wealth should be dealt with. In particular, what is the role to be played by trade unions in redistributing incomes and wealth by means of collective bargaining?

An answer must be found to this question for these developments have profound implications for trade union consideration of any future integrated collective bargaining policy. For it is arguable that, within the accepted framework of recent prices and incomes policy, when great, if rather selective, emphasis was being laid upon the need to eliminate inequities in wage and salary distribution both within and between industries, there were, and still are, powerful institutional forces working towards increasing the existing degree of inequity in the distribution of incomes and wealth rather than, as many hoped, reducing it.

Put simply, workers generally have been and are compelled by the existing economic system to make a contribution, either by direct restraint or, as currently, through higher consumption prices, to the funds available for fixed capital formation. And they do so without having any direct claim whatsoever on the newly created assets. This process of capital accumulation in turn adds to the wealth and the power attached to the owners of existing shares to whom the increased values of the new assets accrue. Licences to print money were clearly in existence long before the creation of commercial television!

In reacting to this situation, trade unions

have always faced a painful dilemma. If they pursue high wage policies as part of their strategy to even up the distribution of incomes and wealth, their actions can be, and are, construed as greedy and inflationary and measures are demanded to reduce their bargaining power. But even where they do gain higher wage levels, they can have no guarantee that employers will not merely raise their prices or reduce sizes or standards in order to protect profit margins, with obvious resultant consequences for real incomes. On the other hand, if trade unions pursue only "moderate" pay settlements, and assuming such policies had no adverse impact on their members' living standards, these would leave the field clear for still greater inequality to be created in the distribution and control of wealth. This dilemma raises issues about the policy options open to trade unions to both reverse this process and give their members a greater say in the control of the new capital.

2. new frontiers in collective bargaining

An adequate and long term solution to this dilemma does not lie in the direction of a return to greater competition, whether in the production and distribution of national resources or in the relatively more restricted area of income distribution covered by collective bargaining. The present Government's neglect of economic planning and its assertions about the virtues of individual self interest as the motivation for social and economic endeavour, are unlikely to solve the nation's basic problems of resource allocation. Nor should they be used as an excuse by trade unions to neglect the scope for collective solutions to our economic and social problems. Indeed, on the basis of post war experience in this country, some commentators take the view that the current lack of a coherent and long term planning policy will at best only defer the need to tackle our deep seated structural difficulties by measures including a greater volume of planned investment. In practice this neglect may well aggravate them still further, making them more intractable for a future administration to solve. More relevant to the theme of this pamphlet, even if a deferment of such problems, albeit temporary, could be achieved by a move back into crude *laissez faire* policies, it would not be an answer which should be acceptable to the trade union and labour movements.

A conception of trade unionism which equated the advancement of workers' interests with the narrow pursuit of purely sectional, economic and social self interest should be and is for many workers utterly alien to the traditions and purposes of trade unionism. If it is anything the trade union movement is collective in both its purposes and its methods and this approach is not limited to the boundaries set by a particular firm or an industry. In any event, as a means of securing changes in the ownership and control of wealth more in favour of working people, the sectional pursuit of gain has clearly not worked any more than the individualistic approach.

So much for the concept, but what about the reality. There is, unfortunately, a basic flaw in some trade unions policies that has led them to place emphasis on the sectional rather than the collective achievement of their bargaining objectives. The fragmented structure of the trade union movement has probably been a contributory factor although this has not prevented unions from pursuing wider social and economic objectives through the TUC. But the less palatable fact cannot be ignored that many workers have come to regard the maximisation of their individual earnings and incomes as their prime objective. In the terminology of economic textbooks, they are concerned with maximising the rate of return on their investment—in this case their labour. In the event, the neglect by unions of their collectivist role in bargaining and the partial achievement of group or sectional well being in some sectors, cannot be said to have helped the overall economic status of workers nor even, it could be argued, the favoured groups themselves.

For it is the sad case that, despite many decades of trade union bargaining effort, the current distribution of wealth and income is still markedly unequal. Moreover, given a continuation of the present Government's fiscal and monetary policies, including the more favourable tax treatment given to higher income groups earlier this year, wealth and incomes are likely to become still more unfairly distributed in the future.

If these trends are to be reversed, a radical answer must be sought within the broad framework of a general attack on poverty and inequality, that is by an attack on social as well as economic injustices. No single policy or strategy could be expected to provide the full answer to the need to bring about effective changes in the distribution of wealth and the concentration of privately owned power in UK industry. The necessary instruments of such a strategy range from more developed fiscal policies through to directly interventionist programmes of reform in industry, including the extension of public ownership and related changes in industrial structures as well as the reshaping to social needs of our educational and training systems. A discussion of all the issues that would arise in the context of such a reform programme would be too wide ranging a task to be dealt with adequately in this pamphlet. These are matters which ought to provide a focus for discussions and decisions within the Labour movement. The clear need now is for complementary policies working in the fields of taxation, social security, education and in the extension of public enterprise.

But, as part of that strategy, there is a need for consideration of alternative ways by which the more advantageous position of the wealth owning minority, and the economic and political influences they wield, can be systematically and permanently eroded by positive, concerted action by trade unions, either acting alone or with some assistance from the State.

For trade unions and their members this requires a consideration of alternative ways of using existing collective bargaining arrangements and, where necessary, the devising of new techniques and policies for operating directly on the structure and ownership of wealth. For the trade union movement itself this may well require a greater degree of centralised co-ordination of wage strategies than has been practiced. Stated briefly, such a move involves providing the means by which—within the framework of a collective bargaining policy agreed to by all trade unions—bargaining policies can be devised and developed with the object of bringing about a fairer distribution of wealth by means of the negotiation of capital funds owned and controlled by trade unions.

Such capital funds would be financed by the firm or industry, they would provide for individual ownership shares for the workers taking part but the funds, which would be used for investment purposes, would be collectively operated by the trade unions concerned.

This linking of trade union activity and wealth redistribution is not a new idea. In its 1968 *Economic review,* the TUC referred to the work of unions in other countries in seeking to establish "within the framework of companies, new categories of corporate funds which would introduce an element of public and workers' rights". A similar theme was expressed in the resolution, approved by the 1970 Congress, which called on the General Council to examine ways by which collective bargaining might be extended to provide for direct trade union ownership and control of self-financed investment assets. This represents clear support in trade union circles for the idea that at least part of the ownership of industrial capital assets should be transferred to funds controlled by workers rather than that they should accrue only to shareholders. A study of the implications is already in hand: the TUC report to the 1971 Congress has stated that the issues which arise from a proposal of this kind are to be studied further by the General Council. Also, the idea is the subject of a capital shares study group of the Labour Party which has been looking, among other proposals, at the ideas put forward by the Danish trade union movement.

Although it would be premature to anticipate the outcome of these studies, a positive recommendation from either the TUC or the Labour Party of schemes for ensuring greater capital democracy would probably be widely welcomed within the Labour movement. For there are many who see distinct advantages to be gained for workers and their organisations in the building up of funds collectively owned and operated on behalf of workers but, at the same time, giving to individual workers a right to a direct share in the ownership of their firm's or industry's capital.

That there is a strong case for the deliberate spreading of capital ownership coupled with the development of financial institutions responsible to workers is no longer in doubt. However, the mere dilution of capital ownership of itself, on lines similar to those advocated by such bodies as the Wider Share Ownership Council, would do little or nothing to create the necessary counterforce to the entrenched power of financial institutions and interests in our country. But such a force could, however, be achieved if, at the same time that workers gained some entitlement to the ownership of capital, this capital were all to comprise a fund which would give the trade unions influence over the acquisition, use and disposal of investment assets. This is the principal object of capital formation funds.

In such a situation, far from being merely the owners of some shares in their enterprise, workers would find themselves, through the medium of trade unions, participating in the control of funds which were used to promote capital formation in their company or industry, but which were ultimately responsible to them. Over a period of time, such funds could become very important financial institutions in their own right perhaps even, as time went on, a dominant factor in the country's economy.

The implications for trade unions and their functions of adding such an element to collective bargaining would be very far reaching. Some of the problems that could arise are fundamental to the role and purposes of trade unions in modern societies. In particular any part played by the State in such arrangements, would need to be considered very carefully so as to avoid any adverse effects on the independence of the trade union movement.

3. West European experience

There is nothing essentially novel in the idea of trade unions involving themselves in securing a re-distribution of wealth by means other than orthodox bargaining over pay and employment conditions. For many years now, political action has been used in this country for achieving these and related aims, although the use of collective bargaining for the purpose of building up capital formation funds would be a step in a new direction for British trade unions. In some West European countries, notably West Germany, Holland, France and Denmark, various schemes have been tried out (see the final report and supplementary report of the OECD regional trade union seminar on "Workers negotiated earnings plans for capital formation", held in Florence, May 1967). These have included investment wages schemes, linking collective negotiations to the individual acquisition of share holdings. An essential purpose and object of these arrangements has been to extend individual share ownership to a wider section of the total population, but especially to workers, in order to secure their participation in the benefits of capital growth. To an outside observer it also seems that an important but subsidiary aim has been to counteract the growing concern in these countries about the concentration of wealth in the hands of a relatively small number of people.

In some of these countries the payment of "investment wages" to workers has come to be regarded as an essential means of bringing about a fairer distribution of wealth. There are significant differences of approach between the various plans designed to achieve this end. Both the German and the French schemes began with legislation which, in the German case gives tax concessions to voluntary, negotiated capital sharing schemes, providing up to roughly £1 per worker per week. Whereas, in the French case, the mandatory capital entitlement is calculated directly from annual profits (after deduction of depreciation, interest and dividends). The common characteristic of these approaches is, however, that they are designed to stimulate and encourage the individual ownership of shares. The West German efforts in particular, which lay emphasis on the role of voluntary collective bargaining, seem to be based on the proposition that the greater the number of people who own shares in private industry as a result of negotiated capital share schemes, the easier it will be to safeguard the institution of private property itself. In more general terms, these can be seen as attempts to avoid the concentration of capital and property which occurs when increased investment is financed largely by higher selling prices of products rather than by broadly based savings.

Perhaps the most attractive proposals yet put forward were announced this year by the Danish trade union national centre (the LO) for a wage earners' national profit and investment fund (see appendix for a summary of this). The main principles may be regarded as a form of general profit sharing since all wage earners, whether employed in public or private industry, would be given a share in the capital growth of industry. Finance for the national fund would be obtained through payments from all employers, beginning with one per cent of their wage bill in the first year and increasing by annual ½ per cent stages up to five per cent. The significant feature of the LO's proposal is that the fund would be trade union controlled and administered, allowing all workers to participate in a form of common ownership through their unions. The objective is to create, through the medium of their trade unions, a means for working people to influence and control capital in industry in much the same way as they influence and regulate pay and conditions of employment. According to the General Secretary of the LO, the Danish employers have felt compelled to respond positively to these proposals by making their own concrete proposals for the introduction of economic democracy.

The Danes have calculated that, after five years, the capital of such a fund would be equal to five per cent of GNP, after ten years 11 per cent, and from the fourteenth year, would level out at 12½ per cent. In our own context, such a proportion of GNP would be about £5,000 million. Given the establishment of such a fund in Britain it could become the single most important source of investment funds in the economy. It would be equivalent to over one quarter of the total wealth held in stocks and shares.

The implications of the development of capital funds for trade union influence over economic decision taking are fairly clear; they would achieve greater worker influence over a wide area of the industries employing them and would go a considerable way towards counteracting inequality in the distribution of the nation's income and wealth.

The West European pattern is, however, a varied one. It ranges from the voluntary negotiated scheme to statutory arrangements; from profit sharing on an individual basis to capital sharing under collective control. There is an obvious area of subjective political choice involved and it is no part of this analysis to pass judgment on such schemes, some of which have the support of radical groups. The form taken in particular countries is related to the structure of their trade unions and the policies they pursue while the relationship between trade unions and the Government is also an important factor.

Their experience and the capital sharing schemes they have put into operation highlight the choice that has to be made between a voluntary or a statutory approach as well as the basic division between individual share ownerships for workers and the creation of collectively operated funds. Choice is, of course, related to the objectives we would wish to pursue in introducing such schemes into our own economy. Although, for our own part, not all British trade unionists would agree that the deliberate fostering of private shareholdings is necessarily a bad thing, it is highly unlikely that the mere wider ownership of shares could bring about a more equal society whilst control of industry is still concentrated in the hands of a relatively small group. The building up of individual employees' shareholdings in such companies as ICI and the John Lewis Partnership (although they are different in kind to the schemes outlined above) indicates that the continental approach is not unknown to our industry. Such schemes are, however, not widespread or popular among British unions. Among the main objections are the tying of monetary improvements to profit movements which are in large part outside workers control and also—very relevant in the current economic climate—the loss of savings involved with fluctuations in share values and the possible liquidation of the company.

Although it is of great interest, West European experience of a statutory approach to capital sharing may not be very helpful to us. For, although it is clearly practicable—as in West Germany and France—to provide tax concessions to encourage such schemes as well as the use of a compulsory scheme in France, there is an important question of the role and attitude of government to be determined. Would British trade unions want to develop their own capital sharing policies on an individual union basis? Would this best be co-ordinated through the TUC or would they support a scheme such as that proposed in Denmark, with the unions playing a dominant part but with powerful support being given by the State to the proposed fund? The answer given by unions to these questions would be a major factor in determining the scope for a statutory approach. If such a scheme as that proposed in Denmark were to be tried out in this country, it would be natural for trade unions to require that it was not a deceptive cover for further interference in wage and salary bargaining, but was rather a positive and tangible step towards achieving traditional trade union objectives of greater equality and economic democracy.

This raises difficult issues about the relationship between unions and the government of the day. Trade unions cannot be certain that governments will be as responsive to the needs and problems of workers as, in the view of unions, they are required to be. The recent experiences of British trade unions in respect of Government statutory intervention could well rule out (at least in the early stages) the likelihood of capital sharing schemes being introduced on a statutory basis.

However, it may well be that such an approach would be pressed on unions because a powerful, perhaps centralised trade union controlled investment fund could strengthen workers' influence, not only on their working environment but also on Government demand management and related policies. The temptation for governments to intervene in the operation of such funds would be a very strong one and legislation would be the means of doing this.

On the other hand, it has to be admitted that it would be simpler to introduce capital funds by means of legislation. It could, for example, help in overcoming any employers objections, enabling a uniform and systematic policy to be developed and extending the advantages of capital sharing to cover all workers both in the public and the private sectors.

Capital sharing schemes introduced by statutory means could be started on a coherent and comprehensive basis and would ensure equal access to such schemes for all workers irrespective of their industry or service. They could also be linked in with other policies designed to secure control over firms' dividend distribution policies and to introduce more developed forms of company taxation.

If a decision were to be made in favour of a statutory approach, there would be much to be said for a scheme based on similar lines to that of the Danish LO. In particular their use of a wages levy to finance the fund would seem an essential feature. If the eventual conclusions of the Labour Party Study Group were to be in favour of some form of statutory support for such schemes, it would be important to include, as a central element, the control by the trade unions of the financial resources secured.

The strengths and weaknesses of reliance on a mainly or wholly voluntary approach must also be noted. Placing the onus for action on trade unions rather than their looking to the State for initiatives, would emphasise the wider collective part they must play in society. This could involve leaving it to unions to originate and develop, as best they could, negotiated capital sharing schemes. How far this would be a practicable approach only experience could show. The opportunities of unions will be different according to their industrial location and their organisational effectiveness. While such an approach would allow considerable scope for experiments with different forms, as their West European counterparts have shown can be done, our own unions could face problems of timing as well as of coverage and operation under a purely voluntary approach.

The negotiation of a limited number of schemes in isolation from the rest of industry would have little effect on wealth distribution. Its purpose would be to provide unions and their members with practical experience in the running of such funds. Negotiating such schemes in the private sector of industry would be at least feasible. For some parts of the public sector difficulties might be encountered, although schemes of this type should not be ruled out in advance. Whether or not workers in the National Health Service, for example, could secure the establishment of a fund giving them greater say in the development of their varied services would be for the trade unions to determine themselves. If it were not feasible, or indeed, if the general experience of voluntarily negotiated schemes produced an unsatisfactory response, perhaps then would be the time to look for a more comprehensive, State inspired system.

On the other hand, capital funds have to start somewhere and, given the uncertainties of securing political action at the present time for a statute based scheme, there is something to be said in favour of trade unions determining what opportunities are available to them in their bargaining with employers. A period of experimentation could well be the best prologue to a subsequent, more ambitious programme based on some form of statutory support. Of course, no guarantee can be given about the likely success of unions in negotiating such arrangements. On the other hand, waiting for the State to assist them has not been a noticeable feature of our trade unions' policies. The interest shown by the TUC in possible arrangements of this kind suggests that their own views may eventually be in this direction and that the debate may soon begin to move away from principles towards the practical details and problems of establishing and operating such funds. It is to these issues that we now turn.

4. establishing capital formation funds

Experimentation implies a number of alternatives. In this section comment is made on one possible approach to the negotiation of capital funds; the setting up of voluntary funds owned by individual members and controlled by their trade unions. The objective in considering this approach is to indicate the scope which currently exists for trade unions to develop a flexible, pioneering approach to these schemes rather than to argue strongly in favour of any one particular method or set of principles.

If the process of establishing the funds were to be entirely voluntary, with no statutory pressure on businesses to share out their wealth, this could well, as already discussed, reduce the scope for forming such funds. In some sectors of the economy, for example in local government, it may be that capital funds could not be started unless there were some statutory underpinning. Nevertheless, there is some scope in both the manufacturing and service sectors of private and public industry. There is no compelling argument against unions securing a recognition of the participative rights of their members in the created wealth of concerns such as ICI, Vickers, BOAC, or any of our other major industrial groups. It would also be particularly useful if unions were to give a high priority to negotiating funds in the larger multi-national companies based in the UK although there is no reason why this policy should be restricted to them. Even companies such as Tesco's and Marks and Spencer's should not be ruled out as candidates. In each individual case the different opportunities for securing agreement on a capital formation fund will need to be explored. In some, the firm's philosophy may lend itself more readily to one being set up. This would seem to be a valid point to be made by unions dealing with firms already carrying out some form of group profit sharing. In other instances, the level of retained profits will be a strong argument for trade unions to use as a justification for conceding a capital formation fund. It would be up to each trade union or joint negotiating body to make what use they could of their available opportunities.

As to the method of establishing capital funds as part of a voluntary collective agreement, this might be as follows. First, negotiations about improvements in pay and related conditions of employment could take place in a normal way with the trade union claim being related in part to the ability to pay, including where appropriate the profitability of the enterprise. At the end of that process there would, in some situations, be a substantial element of retained profits which would normally accrue—either as working capital or as fixed assets—to the company and its existing shareholders. The trade unions' anticipatory response to that situation might normally have been to ensure, either by means of more aggressive bargaining or through better informed claims, that the maximum amount of increased pay was obtained as their members' share of the enterprises' prosperity. From the managements standpoint, a concern with the need to finance new productive capacity or stocks would pull them in the opposite direction of a minimum, limited increase in labour costs. The same conflict situation would exist where, in a strictly commercial sense, no profit was being made (for instance, in the hospital services) but where trade unions' claims were centred in a similar way on the use to be made of limited financial resources.

In these circumstances, it could provide an attractive incentive for trade unionists to accept some measure of trade off as between a bit more on pay or other benefits and some capital sharing arrangement, if it was also agreed that there should be set up, in parallel to an existing wage agreement, a capital formation fund. This could be financed in a number of different ways including sums of money calculated as a percentage allocation either of retained profits or (as in the Danish proposals) of an enterprises' wage costs which it was agreed should be paid into the fund by management. This percentage cash sum—which would be made in addition to the payment of normal wages and salaries—would represent a visible, meaningful transfer of ownership of part of the existing capital assets of the enterprise to employees. In those cases where the contributions were to be paid out of retained profits, this could vary depending on the firm's profit record in any one year. This factor might well influence unions in favour of a percentage allocation related to existing capital assets although fluctuations in the profits contributions could be reduced or avoided by the payment into the funds of minimum or guaranteed amounts. This placing of the emphasis on profit making in order to provide for participation in them would be different in purpose to the mere sharing of profits. It would be the investment uses to which the funds would be put which would be of central importance.

This is not to deny that some managements might see a linking of schemes to profits as a useful means of securing a closer and more committed interest by trade unions and their members in the financial performance of their company.

How far trade unionists would be prepared to go along this road is problematic. But financing arrangements would obviously be a crucial part of any bargained scheme as also would the need for an arrangement to prevent the cost of financing the funds being passed on in the form of higher prices and weakening, as a result, the funds' general redistributive functions.

The general aim of arrangements of this type would be to create funds financed by regular negotiated contributions from profits or payments related to asset values. These funds, representing amounts of money which otherwise might be claimed as wage increases or simply retained by the organisation, would instead become the property of all the income earners covered by the agreement. There is a compelling argument in favour of the creation of individual employees' rights to their share of the fund, for which they would receive certificates which could be encashable after a certain number of years. The creation of such personal ownership rights to a part of the fund would be a necessary feature in order to encourage workers to agree to some part of what otherwise would be their pay or other benefit, taking the form of a share in a capital fund.

The attitudes of individual trade union members would be as crucial to success in setting up capital funds as the attitudes of managements concerned. Individual shares in the fund could be an attractive proposition to some who might see it as a form of deferred benefit but to be realised at the earliest opportunity. Others might, on the other hand, regard their shares as providing, through their trade union's involvement in the funds' operation, for a more direct form of participation in their firm or industry. Where the balance would lie between these views and others hostile to such funds is a matter for conjecture. What is evident is that trade union negotiators would have to convince their members (as they have done with some complicated and sophisticated productivity agreements) about the value of capital funds to them and their union.

Given that, in some situations, such funds could be mutually established, how would they be applied? Here also the precise form of operation could be varied from one situation to another but the principal object would be to use fund resources for investment purposes in the enterprise or for some other form of active investment. These could take the form of loans to the firm for either specific or general investment purposes or the loans might be made outside the enterprise. The willingness of firms to take part in capital funds would probably be affected by whether or not the funds might "escape" in this way and the size of the negotiated payment into the funds might indeed be greater if they were tied to specific firms. However, the recent experiences of Rolls Royce and other companies in financial difficulties illustrates the dangers inherent in this type of arrangement.

Loans from the funds would be made to managements for the purchase of capital assets, such as plant, machinery or buildings. Another purpose could, for example, be the provision of finance for working capital, perhaps even loans to allow production for stock at times of falling demand. In return for the loan the fund's trade union managers would receive back either interest bearing loan stock or shares carrying with them dividends as well as voting rights. The precise form to be taken by the securities given in exchange for investment loans may not be vital: but the rights of fund holders to be consulted about major changes in financial and commercial policy by the company would be clearly established. This would provide the element of control that is the central purpose of capital funds.

Other additional uses might be made of a fund's resources, but before commenting on them it is necessary to outline the possible machinery that will need to be set up by the unions in order to manage their fund. In some cases more than one trade union will be involved and representation on the fund's management committee would need to be proportionate to the number of members represented by each union concerned. Representation would probably best follow arrangements made for joint consultative or negotiating arrangements. Where these joint arrangements did not exist, the coming together of unions to operate a capital fund could be a step in the direction of joint negotiations by fostering common interests and a closer working relationship between them.

Representation on the committee could consist of full time trade union officials and some workplace representatives. The management committee, elected by and, therefore, representing the interests of employee owners of the fund, would need to devise machinery for consulting them and receiving their advice. Its operational function would be to consider proposals by the firm or firms concerned to use monies drawn from the fund for particular investment projects. The management committees' decisions would be subject to advice on the viability of particular investment proposals and it would be an important duty of the committee to secure adequate specialised advice on matters relating to the investment of the fund's assets. This is probably a service that could best be provided centrally in the TUC.

In operating such funds over a period of time, it should be possible to extend their influence beyond the rather static role of merely providing additional liquidity. Borrowers could perhaps be encouraged as a matter of deliberate policy to place shares with the fund as collateral security and perhaps even repay their loans by an exchange of shares for cash. In this way, a direct stake in the ownership of particular companies could be built up by trade unions on behalf of their members. These could considerably strengthen the influence of trade unions over the decisions of management: an influence which is becoming more and more necessary. If the large block of UCS shares owned by the Government had been directly owned by the trade unions concerned, a different situation might have existed than exists today in that part of industry. While not implying trade unionists are some kind of superior management, a more active involvement and interest in that group's affairs, including its dealings with Government departments, could well have alerted the workers and the public to what was being done to UCS.

In addition to these possibilities, the deliberate development of sectoral rationalisation policies would not seem to be inappropriate to a fund's functions, or to trade union involvement in them, enabling the funds to be used to encourage mergers between uneconomic branches of an industry or even buying out uneconomic firms completely. Nor should the objectives of capital formation funds be seen wholly in terms of fostering asset formation or structural changes. The provision of central finance for product and market research or the encouragement of research and development projects which were well beyond the resources of individual companies, could be among the ways by which trade unionists could promote the well being and employment potential of their industries. The closer involvement in the problems of industry that this would entail for trade unions could be a valuable means of extending their influence and responsibilities and could be a move in the direction of workers' control of industry.

Moreover, using the interest charged on capital loans, there could possibly be developed deferred benefits to participants such as pension or annuity payments, death grants or even convalescent facilities. There might even be scope for extending a fund's provisions to include financial assistance towards individual house purchase or the development of co-operative housing schemes for workers concerned. The scope for enlarging the purposes and uses of such funds would seem to be practically unlimited and their effect on industrial relationships could be a very positive one.

Achieved on a voluntary basis, the scale and pace at which capital funds could both be a means of exerting trade union influence on industrial policies and achieving some redistributive effect is clearly unknown. On an annual cumulative basis the value of funds would obviously increase. Their actual rate of increase would, however, depend upon the size of the payment going into the fund each year. If, for example, the Ford Motor Company or Marks and Spencer had agreed to operate such funds during the past ten years, and assuming a five per cent levy on retained profits, the build up of the funds would certainly have varied but would have totalled just under £2 million each at the end of the period. Given the increased capital values during that time, the actual value of such funds would, of course, have been much higher, but the sums involved are still significant for investment purposes.

When measured against the vast inequality set out earlier, the redistributive impact of funds of this size would be limited. Moreover, the restriction of such funds to those industries or firms which conceded them could be regarded as building up privileged groups within the trade union movement. These are strong arguments which could only be met adequately by a comprehensive, statutory scheme. But, as already argued, the case for a voluntary start is essentially one of doing something now to begin the process of setting up funds and accumulating experiences in the practical problems of running them.

But whatever means are chosen for establishing funds there will be a number of problems. One of them is the need for co-ordination of the operation of funds. If there were a centralised fund on the Danish model, co-ordination in investment policy would presumably be easier. The existence of separate industry or firm based funds would require an over view by the TUC of the various possibilities and decisions. Perhaps the TUC will, in its current examination of this issue, make recommendations for a policy on this question. A central investment agency, run by the TUC and representing all the trade unions involved, would seem to be a logical extension of its growing involvement in the collective bargaining policies of affiliated trade unions. Such an agency would also be a powerful instrument in influencing government on its industrial policies.

Other problems include the awkward possibility of internationally mobile capital shunning an area practicing such redistributive ideas as capital funds. This is a problem which relates to the activities of multi-national enterprises generally rather than to an issue specific to the existence of capital funds. If such a movement were to be seen to occur on any large scale it would be for the labour movement to devise additional ways of ensuring that our democratic and national interests were not pushed to one side by such forces. These problems and others concerning the phasing and coverage achieved by such funds would need to be dealt with if a policy of setting up funds were put into effect. It is the idea and the purposes of capital funds which would need to be kept in sight rather than allowing the obvious difficulties to obscure the way to their achievement. Much will depend upon the response and vision of individual trade unions and their members.

5. can unions take on the task?

The preceding outline of possible methods of establishing funds and their potential uses would need to be filled out and fitted to particular circumstances. But the essential feature of the funds would be their provision of a means for securing a growing measure of control over industrial capital by trade unions acting on behalf of their members. The link between democratic control of capital assets through participation in one's union is evident, but there will be those who will question both the willingness as well as the ability of trade unionists to undertake any such new functions.

Reference has already been made to the TUC's own interest in this subject. In addition, there is evidence from the bargaining policies of some trade unions that they are willing to experiment. For example, the creation of the Joint Industry Board (JIB) in electrical contracting by the former ETU has shown how, even in a difficult sector with many small firms and jobs of a relatively short duration, it has been acceptable to trade unionists to broaden their bargaining strategy and to accept a day to day involvement in the employment and related services of the JIB (see *Pay and conditions in the electrical contracting industry*, NBPI report 120). Another instance can be drawn from the steel industry where the existence of worker directors has indicated that workers are willing to accept closer participation in the decisions and responsibilities of their industry.

As to ability, there can be no doubt that the skills of many trade union negotiators who deal with the complexities of modern technology and their impact on workers, are capable of being extended to the making of judgments about industrial loans and investment. As in most things new skills will be acquired by doing the new job. In any event, the assumption that all in management who have such responsibilities are capable of exercising their functions efficiently, but that the representatives of trade unionists would not be able to do this, is a highly questionable one.

This is not to pretend there will be no problems including issues of defective communications between fund representatives and employees. Indeed, given that some move was made towards the setting up of capital sharing funds there would need to be adequate arrangements for consultation as well as, at some stage, co-ordination between the control and operation of particular arrangements. Where a union or unions were involved in a fund's operations, the TUC could agree to co-ordinate their activities, giving specialised advice as appropriate and reviewing progress. Against this background, the case for statutory support of such schemes could be properly evaluated in addition to such problems as those concerned with the longer term effects of confining capital to firms or branches of industry involved with such funds.

Not all the problems that may arise can, of course, be foreseen. It would be up to management and the trade unions to determine the best ways of dealing with them and only practical experience will show whether capital formation funds are a workable proposition in our collective bargaining arrangements. There is, however, nothing to prevent, and much to be said, for trade unions now attempting to negotiate such schemes and for employers to respond in a positive way to their initiatives. For, at a time when there is cynicism in some quarters about the value to society in the functions and purposes of trade uions, it is imperative for both sides of industry to discuss these and related areas of self development. It would be more than a pity if this particular concept, whether based on voluntary negotiations or eventually on statute, were to be neglected in favour of a divisive and, in the long term, damaging, economic and social philosophy.

6. summary and conclusions

If democracy in our society is to be more than a semi-ritualistic participation in infrequent general and local elections, the concept of economic democracy needs to be given a practical application. In particular we need to consider practical ways of involving people in decision making which affects their working lives.

Besides the remoteness that exists between the modern State machine and its citizens, the interests and the working lives of individual workers in modern industry are also in danger of being submerged under the pressures of large scale, often internationally operated, financial interests. Action through the medium of redistributive taxation policies to offset and reduce these pressures can be a valuable means of reducing wealth concentrations, but it is not enough. There is a recognised need for the resources and machinery of collective bargaining to be used to secure both further redistribution as well as some degree of control of industry by workers' organisations.

The main purpose of capital formation funds operated by trade unions is to provide for just this practical involvement in industry, an involvement which workers and their representatives have long aimed for. Choosing investment funds as their point of entry does not preclude action on the extension of public ownership or for worker control of the growing occupational pension funds in industry. Nor should this choice be regarded as an unwholesome involvement with capital which will, in some way, subvert the proper functions of trade unions. Unions are, by their very nature, already involved with capital, dealing with the implications and the consequences of management decisions which affect their members. It is a short, logical and desirable step from this situation to one of establishing more effective control over this decision making process on behalf of their members. Capital formation funds (although not the only alternative) are one means of achieving this.

It is also, perhaps, worth recalling that among the considerations which originally led the trade union movement to support the Labour Government's productivity, prices and incomes policy, was the view that unco-ordinated collective bargaining had made little, if any, impact on the unequal distribution of incomes and wealth, including the distribution of wages, salaries and related benefits between working people. In particular it was felt that more needed to be done to help the disadvantaged, low income groups. There was, in short, strong support among trade unionists for the view that this particular campaign had been fought on too narrow a front and that a different strategy was needed to the tactics of purely sectional bargaining.

scaling down inequalities

This vision still survives though, in the practice of an incomes policy, there was only a limited emphasis on redistribution and even this was seen only in terms of a reallocation of existing rewards between groups of wage and salary earners. That the scaling down of the gross inequalities of wealth distribution between earners and receivers, could not be clearly seen as an integral part of the policy was perhaps its greatest weakness. Capital sharing might have been one way of plugging this gap. It is an idea at least worth trying in any future arrangements that may be worked out in the field of prices and incomes. It is significant that the NBPI, with its long experience of operating a policy based on restraint, recognised the need for a more positive approach when it suggested to the Labour Government that the Board should "undertake a detailed examination of such (capital sharing) schemes as are now being canvassed on the Continent and their relevance to British conditions" (NBPI, *Third annual report,* no 77).

Current Government policies, aimed at slowing down the rise in wages and salaries and reducing the power of unions and their members in bargaining, are not the best background against which to discuss incomes policy questions. Such issues are difficult enough at the best of times, but sooner or later the challenges it poses will need to be taken up yet again and it is important that something is learned from the errors and omissions of the past. A policy which harnessed part of the energy and drive of trade union bargaining to the accumulation of capital formation funds would be a worthwhile experiment. The development of such funds could enhance the position and influence of trade unions and increase the attraction of union membership to workers. They could provide a valuable means for extending concepts of economic democracy within industry while, at the same time, augmenting the nation's resources for productive investment. What is required now is that trade unions and other policy formulators in the Labour movement should lead the way.

appendix

Principles for the creation of a wage-earners' profit and investment fund (as adopted by the LO*'s committee on economic democracy—extracted from the* Danish Labour News, *December* 1970).

1. A wage earners' profit and investment fund should be established by statute to secure to all wage earners, irrespective of their place of employment, a share in the capital growth of society and the yield therefrom.

2. The aims of the fund should be to contribute towards democratisation of the economy, greater equality in the distribution of wealth and income and increased saving, and thus to an increased flow of capital to Danish industry and other important sectors of the Danish economy.

3. The financing of the fund should be effected through the payment of contributions from all employers, private as well as public, at the rate of one per cent of their wage bill in respect of the first year of the scheme, increasing yearly by ½ per cent up to five per cent.

4. The amounts paid into the fund by the employers and the annual income from interest and dividends on capital invested by the fund should be the property of the wage earners. This property right should be secured for the individual through the issue of personal certificates for equal shares in the total capital of the fund.

5. Certificates should be issued in respect of the amounts paid into the fund each year. They should not be convertible, but the individual holder of certificates should be able to redeem the certificates in the fund at any time after a freezing period of five years. Within the five years' period however, redemption should be possible if the holder reaches pensionable age or at the occurrence of death or invalidity.

6. The fund should be an independent institution, working in association with the wage earners' organisations and supervised by the State.

7. In the case of limited liability companies or co-operative societies the entire contribution should remain invested in the enterprise as "responsible wage earners' capital". In other enterprises part of the compulsory payments to the fund may, by arrangement with the fund, remain invested in the enterprise as "special wage earners' capital".

8. In limited liability companies and co-operative societies the wage earners' capital should take the form of shares. In other enterprises the wage earners' capital should be placed before the responsible capital of the enterprise, but after all other commitments.

9. In limited liability companies and co-operative societies the wage earners' capital should have a share in the annual profit on an equal footing with other responsible capital and a pro rata share in the annual growth of the firm's own capital. In other enterprises, interest on wage earners' capital should be paid in accordance with the arrangement made with the fund under section 7; the fund may stipulate an adjustment of the value of wage earners' capital in such enterprises. Yield and interest on wage earners' capital should be paid into the fund at yearly intervals.

10. The wage earners' capital should form the basis of the extension of direct democracy in the enterprises in question. In limited liability companies and co-operative societies the wage earners' capital should be represented on the board by at least one member and by more in proportion to the share of the wage earners' capital in the total voting capital. At the general meeting of a limited liability company or a co-operative society the wage earners' capital should be represented by a number of representatives elected by all the employees of the enterprise in common. Similar rules should apply to enterprises which are organised as companies of a type other than limited liability companies and co-operative societies. In one man firms the wage earners' capital should be represented by the workers' representatives in the joint consultation committee.

11. In connection with the wage earners' profit and investment fund, a special research institute should be established with the task of being at the disposal of the representatives of the wage earners' capital in analysing the accounts and other financial arrangements of the enterprises.

12. In the case of liquidation of an enterprise in which wage earners' capital is invested the wage earners' capital should be transferred to the fund.

13. When a certificate has become redeemable it may at any time be redeemed in the fund at a market value which takes into account the average capital growth since the issue of the certificate and the interest on the total capital of the fund, including wage earners' capital invested in enterprises. The aim of this provision is thereby to secure to all wage earners equal capital growth, irrespective of the type of enterprise in which they are employed and irrespective of their employment being public or private.

14. The portion of the resources of the fund which is not invested in the enterprises as special wage earners' capital should preferably be placed in an active investment, that is in a way so as to obtain a share in the general capital growth and the highest possible yield. Security should be obtained through an appropriate dispersal of investments, for instance on shares, real property and bonds.

15. The fund should be managed by a council composed of representatives of the various organisations of wage earners: the LO, the FTF and others, and by a board of five members, four of which should be elected by the council and one appointed by the State.

16. In association with the fund there should be established local committees and branch committees with representatives of the employees of the enterprises (shop stewards) and of the wage earners' organisations; their task should be to advise in matters relating to the placing of the resources of the fund.